EiM Anthology With Mark Grist
Everyday Superheroes

2025
Billson International Ltd.

Published by
Billson International Ltd
Unit 205,Unit C, 2/F, Kwong On Bank Mongkok Branch Building
728-730 Nathan Road
Mong Kok
Hong Kong
Tel:(852)95619525

Website:www.billson.cn
E-mail address:cs@billson.cn

First published 2025

Produced by Billson International Ltd
CDPF/01

ISBN 978-1-80377-185-4

© Dulwich College Management Asia Pacific Pte. Ltd. All rights reserved.
The original content within this product remains the property of Dulwich
College Management Asia Pacific Pte. Ltd., and cannot be reproduced
without prior permission. Updates and derivative works of the original content
remain the property of Dulwich College Management Asia Pacific Pte. Ltd.
and are provided by Dulwich College Management Asia Pacific Pte. Ltd.
The authors and publisher have made every attempt to ensure that the
information contained in this book is complete, accurate and true at the time
of printing. You are invited to provide feedback of any errors, omissions and
suggestions for improvement.
Every attempt has been made to acknowledge copyright. However, should
any infringement have occurred, the publisher invites copyright owners to
contact the address below.
Dulwich College Management Asia Pacific Pte. Ltd.
101 Thomson Road, United Square, #19-01/03 Singapore 307591

Dear Reader,

Thank you for picking up this year's EiM Poetry Anthology. Whether this is your first time reading one of these collections or you've been following the project for a while, I'm so glad you're here.

This project has grown a lot over the past few years—and this has been our biggest and busiest one yet. We've had more schools involved than ever before, and, for the first time, we're including work from our DUCKS poets alongside those from primary and secondary. The result is a brilliant mix—some poems are bold, some quiet, some hilarious, and some incredibly moving.

Our theme this year, Everyday Superheroes, really struck a chord. Students spent time thinking about who the real heroes are in their lives, and what qualities are actually worth celebrating. Some of the responses were laugh-out-loud funny—especially from our younger writers, who imagined supervillain household objects and unlikely powers. Others turned the whole idea of heroism upside down. And many pieces gave careful, thoughtful insight into what courage, kindness, and strength can really look like in everyday life.

If your work made it into this collection—huge congratulations. This was the most submissions I've ever seen across the EiM schools, and the quality was incredibly high. If you didn't make it in this time, please don't be disheartened—so many brilliant poems just missed out. I'm really grateful to have read your work, and I hope you'll keep writing.

We're always looking for ways to push this project further—and it's been amazing to see how it continues to evolve. This year, the creativity wasn't limited to the page. Across the schools, students responded to the Everyday Superheroes theme through dance pieces, original songs, drama sketches, rap battles, painted portraits, and even VR installations. Dulwich College Shanghai Puxi in particular deserves a special mention for the sheer range and ambition of their work.

One of my favourite additions to the anthology is the audio element. You'll spot QR codes throughout the book—scan them and you'll be able to hear students performing their own poems. It brings a whole new layer to the experience, and I really encourage you to give them a listen. Hearing a young writer bring their words to life in their own voice is something special For the best experience, we recommend to use your phone's own camera application to scan the QR code.

We also ran this year's EiM Poet of the Year competition, judged by the brilliant Theresa Lola and Harry Baker. The standard of entries was incredibly high, and choosing winners wasn't easy. A huge well done to our two highly commended poets:

Rose Z. - "Mortal Wish" (Dulwich International High School Programme Suzhou)

Amelia P. - "Her Hero" (Dulwich College Seoul)

And the biggest congratulations to **Sabina W**. from

Dulwich College Seoul, who became this year's EiM Poet of the Year with her outstanding poem and performance of "Insomnia".

Next year, we'll be coming together in person for our first ever EiM Poetry Festival, which I'm really excited about. But for now, I just want to say thank you—to every student who shared their voice, and to all the brilliant teachers who help make this project such a success every year. And of course, to Jenni Harrison and Edgar Zillmann, whose support and hard work have been essential in making this project happen. There's so much more we can do together—but for now, I hope you enjoy what's here.

These poems are thoughtful, funny, sharp and surprising. They've stayed with me, and I think some of them might stay with you too.

With thanks,

Mark Grist

CONTENTS

13	**A, B, C, D**	Sejun P.
15	**A Robber's List**	Zayn H.
17	**Alarm Clock**	Jiwoo J.
18	**All That I Want**	Elizabeth P.
20	**Am I A Hero?**	Julian P.T.
22	**Angel In White**	Zoe S.
24	**Annoying Clock**	Stella C.
25	**Assessment Stress**	Mia L.
26	**A Villain**	Banby G.
27	**Buzz Lightyear**	Maxton W.
29	**Cat**	Oonagh M.
31	**Colour Pencils**	Barcelona B.S.
32	**Delivery Man**	Minjoon K.
33	**Everyday Heroes**	Alden W.
34	**Everyday Heroes**	Chloe W.
37	**Everyday Heroes**	Joshua H.
38	**Everyday Heroes**	Melissa S.
39	**Everyday Heroes**	Sally L.
41	**Everyday Heroes**	Serena W.
43	**Everyday Superhero**	Alice L.
45	**Everyday Superheroes: My Family**	Arnav C.
47	**Everyday Superheroes**	Colin K.

48	***Everyday Superheroes*** Jack M.	
49	***Everyday Superheroes*** Lauren Z.K. and Violet W.	
50	***Everyday Superheroes*** Nishika S.	
51	***Everyday Superheroes*** Ryder Z.	
52	***Everyday Superhero – Grandma*** William H.	
53	***Everyday Superheroes*** Yuheng X.	
54	***Evil Shower*** Elizabeth C.	
55	***Evil Staircase*** Emily S. and Pepper H.	
56	***Family*** Quan Q.	
59	***Father*** Jojo	
60	***Firefighter*** Jasper L.	
61	***Firefighter*** Lora K.	
62	***Firefighters*** Yewon L.	
64	***Friendship*** Grace S.	
65	***Friendship*** Nick L.	
66	***Gone For Good*** Rachel Y.	
68	***Her Hero*** Amelia P.	
70	***Hidden In Shadows, Samwise.*** Claire P.	
72	***Homework Book*** Seunngu O. L.	
73	***I Am A Firefighter*** Finley B.	
74	***I Am A Mother*** Chantal L.	
75	***I Am A Scientist*** Gavin Z.	
76	***I Am An Everyday Hero*** James Z.	
78	***I Am Kobe*** Anne L.	
79	***I'm Grateful For...*** Alicia	
81	***Imagination*** Linda L.	
83	***Insomnia*** Sabina W.	

86	**Loud, Evil Bell**	Mia K.
87	**Love Yourself? Love Yourself.**	Crystal Y.
88	**Maternal Love**	Josiah Y.
89	**Morning Hero**	Kiki J.
90	**Mortal Wish**	Rose Z.
92	**Mum**	Felix
94	**My Everyday Superhero**	Ahin C.
95	**My Friend**	Martina
96	**My Hero Jane Goodall**	William W.
97	**My Little Brother**	Christine T.
99	**My Mum, The Town's Hero**	Emily K.
100	**My Mother**	Amber
102	**My Superhero**	Paula M.
103	**My Wonderful Brain**	Ruben M.L.
105	**Nurse Suzie & Doctor Brown**	Kira K.
107	**Ordinary Superhero — Chocolate**	Joanna Q.
109	**Paper Villain**	Lumi L.
110	**Pencil Sharpener**	Jonathan S.
111	**Police Officers**	Hanwen L.
112	**Rude Sneaky Shower**	Annie K.
113	**Smile**	Julie J.
114	**Superhero**	Aurora H.
115	**Superhero Next To Me**	Chanel C.
116	**Sweeper Of The Night**	Rowan T.
118	**Teacher**	Sarah Z.
119	**Terror**	Isaac H.
120	**The Book**	Julia S.

121	***The Day Kindness Came To Visit***	Lucas
123	***The Day That Bravery Came To Visit***	Elsa
126	***The Door Holder***	Neil A.
127	***The Evil Rubber***	Lyra J.
129	***The Family's Embrace***	Andrea R.
130	***The Heroes That Walk With Us***	Michelle B.
131	***The Ring***	Cheawon L., Joy B. and Seoyun J.
132	***The Saviour Of The Stomach***	Cindy Z., Sally L. and Zoe H.
133	***The Window***	Andrew L.
134	***They Were Everything To You***	Theo G.
136	***To Be Kind***	Amy Y.
137	***Upstanders***	Isabel L.
141	***War***	Elizabeth S.
142	***Way***	Felix K.
143	***Xi'an***	Hannah S.
144	***Yes Indeed, Things We Need***	Horace G. and Martin Z.
145	***Your Own Hero***	Liya D.

A, B, C, D

A, B, C, D is all it says,

a hand, a pen, and four circles,

its presence makes me daze,

bewildered with a burst of berserk here and there,

an inch away from insanity, I possibly am.

Pencils (they roll), rubbers (they're stationary), and the ruler (it... exists)

all cavort graciously in a harmonious overture to a reality check,

while my eyes instead drift to the queue of Cs that I see all too much.

C,

C,

C,

See this for yourself:

Once again, I evoke my mind,

a trailblazing method to all A+ students,

a truly intriguing "theory of everything"

that beholds the boundaries of possible and impossible,

a failing student's last stand, yet

an answer determined by the prophecies of fate.

I count: 1, 2, 3. Deep breath.

A, B, C, D is all it says,

A hand, a pen, and four circles.

With an assurance and valor like never before,

the tip of graphite meticulously embroiders a metallic grey circle,

And my decision is immaculate. A it is.

I got it wrong.

Sejun P.
Dulwich College Seoul

A Robber's List

List of things I've stolen:

A child's small dog, and its bright-eyed stare,

A widow's tears, a heavy care,

A baker's yeast, a rising fear,

The whispered secrets, held so dear.

A barber's shears, a tangled mane,

A painted landscape, sun-kissed rain.

A scholar's quill, a half-writ rhyme,

A stolen moment, out of time.

A firefly's gleam, a summer's sigh,

A sailor's compass, 'neath the sky.

A newborn's laugh, a fragile sound,

The very silence, underground.

A silver locket, memories cold,

A rising dread, a story told.

A flat screen TV, a flickering light,

A roast hog's feast, in darkest night.

A swinging tree, where joy once flew,

A stolen life, it's sadly true,

A hollow soul, what can I do?

Zayn H.
Dulwich College Seoul

Alarm Clock

Wakes me up. Pulls me out of sleep.
Never tired. Never quiet.

Stops me from being late and saves my day.
Without it, I'd miss the bus. I'd miss school.

Always too loud. Always too early.
Some days, I want to throw it away.

But still, it does its job.
Keeps me on time.
Even if I hate it sometimes.

Jiwoo J.
Dulwich College Seoul

All That I Want

All that I want,

Is to be by your side.

All that I want,

Is to match your stride.

Hit me like a ray of sun,

Burning through my darkest nights.

You protect me with your toy gun,

And I'm addicted to your light.

Call me when you get lost,

'Cause I just wanted you to know,

That if our paths never crossed

I would've never said hello.

You save me from doubt,

Without you I'm down in the dumps.

You carry me through the dark,

You're my hero when hope just slumps.

All that I want,

Is to be by your side.

All that I want,
Is to match your stride.

Elizabeth P.
Dulwich College Shanghai Pudong

Am I A Hero?

Am I a hero? Am I a villain?
Look through my feelings
What are you seeing?
Do you see millions or billions
Of different moments shaping my life?

You could see the villain, the bad side
The rude and evil, the mischievous
I am a sinner, describe me, perfidious
A malice with no mercy and pride
And an eye out for prey and out for the hunt

Or you could see a hero within
A kind and charismatic one-of-a-kind
The side of me that is benign
The one that looks with a happy grin
And a look in his eyes of compassion

Some say I'm a caring champion

Others say I'm a crooked scoundrel

Bipolar but I'm not a bounder

Look at me, an all-rounder

Fighting myself, am I a hero?

Julian P.T.
Dulwich College Seoul

Angel In White

In the mayhem of battles where shadows collide,
the cries of anguish are full of pain,
the crimson stream which fills the river,
Bearing witness to loss, to sorrow and more.

Within the pain, an angel steps forth as her white figure
beams in the dark.
With gentle hands she soothes the pain,
She heals the wound, stitch by stitch.

Each life she touches, another soul will be saved,
With kindness like a ray of sunshine,
It leaves an imprint in their hearts.

Her presence crackled like a bonfire,
"Mother I'm scared"
With gentle flutter, her wings embraced the boy
"Don't worry son, I'm here for you."

Zoe S.
Dulwich International High School Programme Hengqin

Annoying Clock

I am a noisy, annoying alarm clock.
I wait until morning,
Touching the cold, hard, wooden table all night.
I always hear loud snoring in the peaceful room,
And I taste the dust in the smelly air.
I feel the strong wind crushing my face.

But there is more to me than that!
I am a supervillain!
And I am here to wake the whole house!
I will wake the people with my noisy sound
And the humans will wake right up.
The humans will BEG me to stop,
And jump out of bed.
The whole house will be MINE!
And I will feel...
GLAD, happy!

Stella C.
Dulwich College Suzhou

Assessment Stress

Numbers and lines,

Circles and letters –

Shaping a path, as if it matters.

Sitting at a desk,

Dreams suppressed,

Working to death

Just to determine where you would work till your last breath.

Is this the measure of life's worth?

A cycle unbroken since our birth.

Trapped by a system defining our Earth.

Where's the freedom we were told to find?

Lost in a maze of the world's design.

Mia L.
Dulwich College Suzhou

A Villain

Village harbors a repulsive man,

Inflicting harm on many within.

Legions of folks loathe this man,

Lies have perpetually shadowed him.

Anxiety lingers heavily here,

Insulting numerous villagers, as well.

Notoriety stains his dwelling place.

Banby G.
Dulwich International High School Programme Hengqin

Buzz Lightyear

Plastic, plastic, plastic. Everything is plastic.
Everything is fake, so can I just say,
"If anything happens to you, it's not that drastic;
These things happen in life, you'll always find your way."

Even when your friends don't laugh but smirk,
And all the stuff that they say hurts.
In the end, stay strong.
Stay on track.

When my dog passed
They once asked:
"Did you eat your dog,
did you feed him to the hogs?"
Words can destroy, words can kill;
Words can make everybody feel
Pain, strife, injustice. They can make people kneel.

But keep your chin up son,
It always gets better.
When sadness comes, run.
Don't be scared, you're a go-getter!

Don't let the flame inside you die

Or else darkness will dawn.

As the legendary Buzz Lightyear once cried,

To infinity and beyond!

Maxton W.
Dulwich International High School Programme Hengqin

Cat

My cat is evil,

He makes mischievous schemes.

In the layer he scrapes the litter,

But it is not as in seems.

His thick ginger fiery coat

Has layers upon layers of deceit at its best.

CRASH

                                                        PING

                CRACKLE

                            BOOM

Oh no - what are those fumes...

Hopefully just some fried legumes.

My cat was ginger, a shadow now,

Later, he leapt and dove at tiny flies

Teasing him at the window high

We laughed, we giggled.

But that stare he gave seemed ever so chilling,

But at the end of the day,

Brushing my teeth.

I hear a slight sound,

Quite near my feet.

I know what he wants,

My buzzing brushing machine.

I kneel to him as he chews,

At one end of my gadget for teeth.

Oonagh M.
Dulwich College Seoul

Colour Pencils

We are colourful colour pencils

We lie against your box every day

We see your new paper we want to squeal about

We want to hear you say, "Yay it's colouring day!"

We're getting closer

We can smell your fresh paper, yay

Red, yellow, blue, green, purple and orange

Good choices but there's more to me than that

We are secret superheroes

We'll colour all your blanks

Aw it's time to say goodbye

Oh well, see you the next day!

Barcelona B.S.
Dulwich College Seoul

Delivery Man

Slave

That is what I think of my life cycle

I think I am nothing but a slave with a helmet and a motorcycle

Slave

That sounds like me

I don't think I have right of liberty

Nor equality

I just have to deliver things to people

To those I think are more powerful than me

Even though we are totally equal

Please be grateful for me.

Minjoon K.
Dulwich College Suzhou

Everyday Heroes

Dark night. All asleep.

No light. Counting sheep.

You keep us safe.

So we can rest.

Dear policeman,

You are the best.

Raging fire. Heavy smoke.

Not a liar. Not a joke.

Risks his life to save us all.

Dear firefighter,

Wish you never fall.

Alden W.
Dulwich College Beijing

Everyday Heroes

Everyone can be an everyday hero,
Maybe you can too.
You might have just not noticed it,
You just need to break through.

You might be wondering what an everyday hero is,
Let me tell you now.
They don't even wear a cape,
But they are a hero somehow.

An everyday hero is brave,
They always help everyone.
They always face challenges that are scary,
And they always have caution.

An everyday hero is kind,
They help people who are lonely.
They share with lots of friends and family,
And they treat everyone nicely.

An everyday hero has resilience,
They never give things up.

They are always helping others cheer,
And they aim for the top.

An everyday hero does teamwork,
They always help each other.
Every day and every night,
They are facing challenges together.

An everyday hero makes sacrifices,
They always put others in front of them.
They help save children from dangerous situations,
Even if they will lose a thumb.

A nurse can be one,
A police officer can be one.
A firefighter can be one,
They can all be everyday heroes.

Everyone can be an everyday hero,
Maybe you can too.

You might have just not noticed it,
You just need to break through.

Chloe W.
Dulwich College Shanghai Puxi

Everyday Heroes

Selfless hearts, with quiet grace,
Brave in every challenge they face.
Resilient souls through highs and lows,
They shine as everyday heroes.

Their acts of care, both small and grand,
Shape the world with a steady hand.
No need for glory, no need for fame,
Their selfless courage earns the name.

Joshua H.
Dulwich College Shanghai Puxi

Everyday Heroes

Heroes don't simply become heroes

At first, they are but a speck of light, lost in darkness.

Then they become a dot of illumination

A blob of potential

A figure taking shape,

At last, standing tall, a giant of positivity,

Shining fierce and bright.

A fire of hope gleams in their eyes,

A hope to change the future, a selfless act.

Everyday heroes shine brightly in others' lives.

But remember,

They all come from a single speck of light.

Melissa S.
Dulwich College Shanghai Puxi

Everyday Heroes

When you ask an everyday hero if they are a hero, they will say no.
But when you ask a superhero if they are a hero, they will say yes.
An everyday hero will just be kind and normal,
They'll wear no cape, just a T-shirt and a smile,
Helping others with kindness, going the extra mile.

They might be a teacher who inspires young minds,
Or a neighbor who helps when trouble unwinds.
A friend who listens when you're feeling down,
Or a stranger who lifts you when you wear a frown.

Then there are the firefighters, brave and strong,
Rushing to help when things are wrong.
With courage and teamwork, they fight the flame,
Saving lives every day, without seeking any fame.

Even the guard at the gate might be a hero,
How many times did he sleep or rest: zero.
A hero might be a friend, who raised money for charity,
That friend might be the one who always loses Monopoly.

They don't seek glory or shine in the light,
But their actions speak volumes, they make the world bright.
With courage and heart, they quietly lead,
Planting the seeds of compassion and good deeds.

And let's not forget about ourselves,
You could become one, without any spells.
You did something that seemed like the right thing to do,
And before you know it, that hero is you.

Sally L.
Dulwich College Shanghai Puxi

Everyday Heroes

They are often ignored,
Not noticed,
Brave, yet underrated.
But they are the people that help us create a good life
And not even asking for gratitude from others.
Who are they?

They are selfless, ordinary, calm, and they work hard.
They are a group of people that help create the world that we live in
They are OUR everyday heroes.

Everyday heroes come in all shapes and sizes,
From nurses, to firefighters,
From parents, janitors.
These people are the reason why the world is how it is.
They help us when we are in need,
Fight for us when we need to be freed.

They show dedication to their work, at home or in foreign places,
Where for most people, the stress encases.

They show compassion, showing kindness to everyone around
No matter where they came from, no matter their background.
They show resilience, facing challenges like us,
Both mental and physical, without making a fuss.
They show courage, risking their lives,
But they'd be willing to put up a fight.

Moms, dads, janitors, policemen,
They are human, in different forms.
They have their fair share of challenges as well.
Emotional stress, dangerous conditions,
Separation from family etc.

Remember, not all heroes wear capes,
Most of them are just hiding in plain sight!

Serena W.
Dulwich College Shanghai Puxi

Everyday Superhero

In a crowded subway station, a girl lost her way.
Separated from her mother, on that terrible day.
Clenched hands, now pulled apart.
She was overwhelmed by the crowds, with a broken heart.

The door slowly closed, making a dreadful sound.
Fear and panic were all around.
She screamed out loud in despair.
Her eyes, brimming with tears, resembled a leaky tap that had not been repaired.

Then, a strong figure came.
He patted her on the back, as her mother did the same.
"Your mother will return," he softly said.
These warm and powerful words, calmed down her head.

Soon enough, her mother rushed back.
Instantly, a snug embrace they did not lack.
She saw the boy get up and away, through her blurry eyes.
He left quietly, just like an unsung hero hardly being recognized.

Tears rolled down, her vision cleared.
His kindness, lighting up the darkness, always there.

Kindness gives everyone the power to be a hero.
Because of kindness, there are things we can handle more than just a little.
Because of kindness, anyone can be the everyday superhero.

Alice L.
Dulwich International High School Programme Hengqin

Everyday Superheroes: My Family

Time and time again,
I find my ears ringing like a bell.
I don't like it, I don't like it at all,
I wish it would fade, I wish it would quell.

That's when I turn to my everyday superheroes,
The ones who stand by me through highs and lows.

My family
My father, my mother, my sister,
Always there to help and guide.
From little worries to the biggest blisters,
With love and patience by my side.

They don't have superpowers,
Oh no, they don't,
But all superheroes don't need powers,
Just strength to face what others won't.

A hero is anyone willing to care,
Anyone honest, brave, and fair.

Anyone who puts you in front of themselves,
Giving their love before anything else.

That's what my family is to me,
Though from afar, it may not seem.

Arnav C.
Dulwich College Shanghai Pudong

Everyday Superheroes

The clueless, coolest but toothless, corner shop man.
His horrible jokes, English and tricks never good or okay just horrible, his goof
Never stops, he's so unfunny makes me burst out crying of second-hand embarrassment.
His cheap yummy gummy never disappoints my grumpy tummy and transforms me into a dummy.
He's balder than a bald eagle but eager to be richer then Jeff Bezos
His eyes are filled with black, his head is filled with nothing but a heart for jokes
Bossman will always be on top and me top customer
I will always remember that time when I forgot to pay
And he said it's fine and I gave it the next day
I'm grateful for this bossman.

Colin K.
Dulwich College Seoul

Everyday Superheroes

Everyday heroes, their powers unseen,

No flashy suits, no silver sheen.

Teachers shaping futures bright,

Nurses heal through the night.

Parents guiding with gentle care,

Drivers steady through wind and rain,

Friends who help a heart's pain.

Through humble acts, their strength they show,

The everyday heroes we all know.

Jack M.
Dulwich College Shanghai Pudong

Everyday Superheroes

I love Gummy.

Gummy loves me.

Gummy eats shark

But the sharks don't sanitize

So gummy throws whiteboard pens at his mom

Gummy always cries for his sins

So Gummy prays

Whenever he finishes praying he eats hairbrushes

But Gummy doesn't have teeth

So Gummy knows it's a sin

Gummy is a sinner

Gummy ate the building I fell off of

Gummy is no longer a sinner

Gummy is now my superhero

Everyone loves Gummy

Who doesn't love Gummy?

Lauren Z.K. and Violet W.
Dulwich College Seoul

Everyday Superheroes

They don't wear capes or fly through the sky,

No laser beams flashing from their watchful eye.

No comic book stories, no headlines in red,

But they save the world with kind words instead.

The teacher who stays long after the bell,

Helping a child learn to read, learn to spell.

The nurse who holds a trembling hand,

Whispering, "You're strong, you'll soon stand."

The parent who works the night shift again,

Sacrificing sleep just to make sure they win

Not trophies or medals, but food on the plate,

A roof overhead, and love that won't break.

The stranger who stops when the rain pours down,

Sharing an umbrella in the middle of town.

The friend who listens when words start to crack,

Who carries your burdens when you can't hold them back.

Not all heroes wear armor of steel,

Some fight battles no one can feel.

With kindness, with courage, with hearts open wide,

They change the world, standing right by our side.

Nishika S.
Dulwich College Seoul

Everyday Superheroes

A nurse, with a magic touch so nice,

Heals injuries with warm tea and time.

A teacher, as patient as can be,

Makes learning fun, for you and me.

A firefighter can save cats from trees,

And putting out fires with such ease

Parents who keep everything in line,

With a heart full of love that's always on their mind.

These everyday heroes, no capes in sight,

Only hearts of gold, making things right.

Ryder Z.
Dulwich College Shanghai Pudong

Everyday Superhero – Grandma

My hero doesn't fly,

But she always finds my socks when they're gone.

My hero doesn't wear a cape,

But she fixes Jiao-Jiao when something's wrong.

She doesn't fight bad guys with laser beams,

But makes yummy dumplings, round and warm.

Her love gets bigger every day,

She's my grandma. I love her so much.

William H.
Dulwich College Beijing

Everyday Superheroes

Behind shadows, where quiet deeds are done,
Lie powers unseen, like rays of morning sun.
No fancy costumes, nor ability to fly,
Yet everyday superheroes, walk humbly in disguise.
We live in a world where kindness lights the way,
You can be the dawn that turns night to day.
A simple smile, or a hand to hold, (no big deal),
Becomes the sparkle that makes bad vibes kneel!
We live in a world where worries hide,
You can be the joy that turns the tide.
A steady voice, a meme, or a hilarious joke,
Can save the day better than a superhero's cloak!
We live in a world where hope feels kinda cheap,
You can be the drummer that maintains the beat.
With every force, but treating with care,
You're basically Batman, but with way better hair.
No cape or mask, just courage and grace,
It's just everyday heroes that make the world a better place.

Yuheng X.
Dulwich College Shanghai Pudong

Evil Shower

I am an evil shower.

I stand in front of you.

Touching the clean water.

Each day I see people and germs.

I hear loud, creepy water.

I feel the salty water and I taste yucky germs.

I am a supervillain!

If you turn the water to cold,

I will turn the water hot then…

EEEEEESSSSSSSAAAAAAA!"

Fantastic!

Elizabeth C.
Dulwich College Suzhou

Evil Staircase

I am a mean, evil flight of stairs.

I lie in the corridor touching the cold, wet carpet.

Each day I see plastic plants fall on me and people walk on me.

I hear the noisy vacuum cleaner on my face.

I feel the carpet on top of me and taste the stinky air.

But there's more to me than that...

I'm here to injure some people!

I will injure humans,

and they will go to hospital!

The humans will never dare to walk on me,

and run on me – NEVER.

The whole house will fear me, and I will feel...

Happy.

Emily S. and Pepper H.
Dulwich College Suzhou

Family

I'm grateful for my family
They are friendly and they are fun
They make sure that I wear a coat
But they also give me hope.
They help me to fly my kite
From the safety of my home.

I'm grateful for my family
They care about me, give me energy.
When I am annoyed they give me joy.
When everything is but, but, but
They never leave me outside
With the front door shut.

I'm grateful for my family
I'd be lonely if they weren't here,
Brothers and sisters are annoying
But please don't disappear
I wonder sometimes if
My parents are as happy as me
If they ever feel it is a lot of work
To keep such a strong family

I hope they are happy to care about us.

Because I am grateful for our family.

Quan Q.
Dehong Shanghai International Chinese School

Father

To me, you are sugary apple juice,
because you give me energy.
Sometimes you are a cute puppy, because you warm me up
when I am sad.
You are the smell of a rose,
both gorgeous and royal
and the sound of a helpful bird
chirping beside me
sharing such good ideas.
You are the pride I feel
when I help a friend solve a problem.
You are a secret door
that keeps me safe
and lets me hide inside.
You are two pounding
giant mountains
ready to block any danger from me.
You always keep me safe behind you.
Best of all,
you are my father.

Jojo
Dehong Shanghai International Chinese School

Firefighter

Prometheus brought us the fire
but also brought us the monster.

We need someone to stop the creature

So the Savior has come into the world
They are not a god; they are not eternal

They stop tears of suffering from the fire in hell
and steal people from the Grim Reaper.

They helped mankind
but they can't help themselves.

Jasper L.
Dulwich College Suzhou

Firefighter

Why are you screaming all over the night?

Are you burning so brightly to light up this night?

Or are you burning so hot to warm this night?

What are you so angry about?

What are you so upset about?

We try to soothe and calm you down

Then you become quiet as if nothing had happened

Why were you screaming all over the night?

Lora K.
Dulwich College Suzhou

Firefighters

When the earth shakes and the skies turn gray,

And fear tries to take our hope away,

Fearless footsteps on dangerous paths

Walk through fire to carry others out

No hero's cape, no shining sword,

They keep moving forward into the blaze

As their courage burns brighter,

The flames slowly fade away.

Yewon L.
Dulwich College Suzhou

Friendship

I used to have a best friend.

But not anymore.

She used to listen to me and hang out with me.

Before she met them.

Ever since she became close friends with them,

She started to be mean and left me out.

She started to say bad things about me.

Dozens of eyes were towards me,

I could hear them whisper.

I tried my best to tell the truth

But no one listened to me nor understood.

I was losing hope.

I started to lose my smile and the motivation of coming to school was gone.

But then, I met her.

She was different from others.

Grace S.
Dulwich College Suzhou

Friendship

Friend: a person who leads me to escape from darkness.

Friend: a person who can cancel out my loneliness.

Friend: a person who can help my study progress.

Friendship is like a bridge that links our hearts.

Friendship is like an umbrella over our hearts.

Nick L.
Dehong Xi'an School

Gone For Good

I remember when...
The first touch was soft, he was fluffy and small, with white and brown fur.
He explored everything in his path, without any doubt.
He's a puppy, we named him Rico, rich in Spanish.
I stared into his dark eyes, while he was messing with his toy,
It was full of mystery, it must be a great adventure with the boy!

I remember when...
I had to go to a summer camp, and saying goodbye was hard
I told him we would play again...
And I trusted my instincts.
After the camp, our family went on a trip.
It wasn't long, only five days till I'd see him again!

I remember when...
One day, it was raining
Not those heavy ones, it was quite soft
That morning, our family had to stay inside, nothing would go wrong...
Right?

Suddenly, my mom stood up with a phone call, facial expression hardening
After it finished, I asked, "What happened?!" She wouldn't answer
Until I asked again, she said, "Rico's gone for good…"
I remember when…
I let the message flow through, a sudden BANG in my head
HOW could that be POSSIBLY TRUE?!
Hundreds and millions of questions popped out of my head
I knew there was only one answer:
ADMIT IT.

I remember when…
Tears started to flow down my cheeks, that CAN'T be!
ADMIT IT.
I cried all night, flipped and flopped, just couldn't sleep
Oh! The hurt was too deep! There must be some mistake!!!
ADMIT IT.

Now…
I remember Rico not only as a good boy…
But a hero that would lighten everyone's days!

Rachel Y.
Dulwich College Suzhou

Her Hero

Her practised smile gleams,
Beaming to the world, yet
Never quite reaching her eyes

Her steps fall sharp and sure,
Measured grace they all admire, yet
Each one is heavy with what she hides

Because behind the scenes,
She comes undone,
Her intricate disguises peeled off one by one

"No one understands," she claims,
But how could they hold unoffered hands?
She presents them an act, then begs them to see
The soul that trembles beneath the plea.

"They need to accept me," she cries,
But what if 'they' really is 'I'?
No soul can reach what has not been shown
No one can love what has never been known.

Maybe she needs to stop the game,
Stop dimming herself to fit the frame
The love she chases, the peace she seeks,
It whispers loud, but the voice is weak

She awaits her hero, her savior, her hope, as she bleeds,
But perhaps it is herself that she truly needs.

Amelia P.
Dulwich College Seoul

Hidden In Shadows, Samwise.

You walked in shadows, by his side,
Through darkened paths where hope has died.
A simple gardener, brave and true,
With courage found in all you knew.

You carried burdens, light and heavy,
Through endless roads, dark and dreary.
The weight of friendship in your hands,
You journeyed through the broken lands.

When the fire burned too bright,
You never once gave up the fight.
For Frodo, the world, for all,
You answered every little call.

So here's to you, the quiet guide,
The steadfast hero by his side.
Because deep down you always knew,
The strength was found in love so true.

Claire P.
Dulwich College Seoul

Homework Book

I am a naughty homework book.

I sit on a table and touch a pencil.

Each day, I see a child getting dizzy and making him dizzy.

I hear a child say: "Aaaaaagh!"

I feel the child being bored,

and taste easy and hard questions.

But there's more to me than that.

I am smart and naughty.

And I'm here to help learning and make people dizzy.

I will send away the playful and kick out the joyful.

The humans will be bored of me and hate me.

The whole house will say, "I don't like homework!"

And I will feel grateful.

Seunngu O. L.
Dulwich College Suzhou

I Am A Firefighter

I am brave and strong.

I wonder how many fires I can stop.

I hear the fire crackling.

I see houses burning.

I want to save as many people as possible.

I am brave and strong.

I pretend I am a god and that I can save everyone.

I feel upset when people get hurt.

I touch the fiery door.

I worry about people's lives.

I cry when people die.

I am brave and strong.

I understand that people could be having a hard time.

I say nobody should give up on their dreams.

I dream for everybody to be safe.

I try to help everyone.

I hope that I don't let anyone down.

I am an everyday superhero.

Finley B.
Dulwich College Shanghai Pudong

I Am A Mother

I am a mother that cooks every day and is busy every day.

I wonder has anyone been this busy before?

I hear that being busy is a good thing for women.

I see that being busy is hard and tough.

I want calm, comfort and communication.

I am a mother that cooks every day and is busy every day.

I pretend that I am relaxed.

I feel misunderstood but happy to be.

I touch bowls, pans and cups.

I worry that my child will not be brave.

I cry sometimes but not so much.

I am a mother who cooks every day and is busy every day.

I understand empathy, emotions and happiness.

I say thank you to myself and everyone.

I dream for comfort, calm and positivity.

I try to do everything that is challenging and tough.

I hope that someone can assist me.

I am an everyday superhero at home and in the future.

Chantal L.
Dulwich College Shanghai Pudong

I Am A Scientist

I am a scientist.

I wander through the forest, searching for ripe knowledge.

I hear waterfalls of opportunity.

I see ideas leaping and flying.

I want to bring back an idea.

I want to see it flourish.

I feel the seeds are growing.

I touch blooming ideas.

I worry for the forest's opportunities.

I cry when a knowledge-filled flower withers.

I am a scientist.

I am an everyday superhero.

Gavin Z.
Dulwich College Shanghai Pudong

I Am An Everyday Hero

Everyday heroes, who are they, who are we?
Hidden among us, they fight for our survival,
Although uncredited.

A two-star general, brave and wise,
An everyday hero beneath the skies.
They face tough choices, fate in their hands,
Yet find joy in peace and the strength of their bands.
With each mission fulfilled, their legacy grows,
In laughter and honor, their duties fulfilled

A firefighter, resilient and dedicated,
An everyday hero beneath the blaze.
They face flaming buildings, lives in their hands,
Yet they find light in unity and purpose.
With every tragedy, comes a life of resilience,
In courage and valor, life's hazards discarded.

A spy, silent and secret,
An everyday hero beneath the river of truth.
They face chases and interrogation,
Their country's secrets in their hands.

Yet, they find hope in the realm of the hidden,
With every success, their footprint rises.

We are everyday heroes.
We do not do it for the credit,
We do it for the greater good.
Hidden among the public,
A silent influence.
No matter who you are,
Whenever you need us,
We are always there.

James Z.
Dulwich College Shanghai Puxi

I Am Kobe

I am Kobe.

I wonder if my family is okay.

I hear people crying.

I see pain in the USA.

I want to come back.

I am Kobe.

I feel love for my fans.

I worry about my family.

I cry in heaven.

I am Kobe.

I understand your pain.

I say don't be sad.

I dream to hug Capri.

I hope she will be happy.

I am Kobe Bryant.

Anne L.
Dulwich College Shanghai Pudong

I'm Grateful For...

I'm grateful for my mum,
Her love unfolds with each new dawn,
Cooking, cleaning until my heart is won
With a smile that shines like the sun
Earning money through the days
She helps me survive in many ways,

I'm grateful for our doctors,
Careful hands, swift and sure,
Healing pain, finding a cure
Long hours that they endure.
Minds so sharp and hearts so pure.

I'm grateful for our police.
For all that they do
Superheroes dressed in blue,
Doing what's right, fearless and true.
Protect and serve their oath in view.

As we go through life, such heroes we find
With love and care they touch our lives.
Learn from examples, the things they do
Perhaps you could be a hero too.

Alicia
Dehong Shanghai International Chinese School

Imagination

The thunder roars, which sends my heart pumping.

It strikes and makes my body frozen,

Breaking through the heavenly tribulation, I laugh as a king.

Changing my fate against the heavens, I yelled, "Yippee!"

Now time for reality and to go to the cinema and watch my movie.

Linda L.
Dehong Xi'an School

Insomnia

At night I lie awake
Alone in my bed
As these terrible thoughts
Consume my head

Do you know what it is
Corrupting my dreams?
Do you know what it is
Preventing my sleep?

I cannot find rest
There's just too much noise
Too much going on
Can't focus on one voice

Insomnia.
Insomnia
In so
   m ni a

Doctors speak of it
Like a disease

But I know what it is
It's my arch-enemy

I toss and I turn but it's
Stealing my nights
My thoughts swirl and twirl
Diminishing my light

I'm unfocused and lazy
During the day
If only they knew
I've so much to say

And then I was saved.

A knight in shining armour
Caffeine came to me
In coffee and tea
In all of its glory

Though I could walk
A bounce in my step
For some reason my smile
Was still being kept

Sure I had energy
But with it came
A short temper, a hot head
Even more pain

My hero had turned
Me into a monster
I no longer had patience
My heart beats even faster

Yes sleeping is hard
But caffeine was no fun
So now I am back
All the way to square one.

Sabina W.
Dulwich College Seoul

Loud, Evil Bell

I am a loud, noisy bell.

I live on the sticky kitchen shelf.

Touching warm, wet hands and cold plastic shelves.

Each day I see sleepy people on the sofa.

Even on the beds and carpets.

I hear a quiet house and then... snoring.

Loud, ugly snoring!

I feel sticky hands wrap around my shiny bell,

And taste the cold morning air.

But there is more to me than that...

I am an evil villain,

And I am here to... WAKE UP THE HOUSE!

RRRIINNGGGGG

And will feel,

SATISFIED!

Mia K.
Dulwich College Suzhou

Love Yourself? Love Yourself.

You see it every day,
in the mirror, in the water.
You feel the way it does,
as if you were it.

What is it?
Might you question yourself.
You need it, just as
it needs you.

You may love it, or you
may hate it. It saves you,
when you are blue,
its hands grasp for you.

You don't thank it,
or rarely you do.
Shall you appreciate it?
You are it; it is you.

Crystal Y.
Dulwich College Shanghai Pudong

Maternal Love

When I was little, mother's hug,
This is maternal love.

Growing up, the company of friends,
This is friendship.

Grown ups, a passionate kiss,
This is love.

However,
Friends fly away and leave in time,
Lover is hopefully eternal, but easily broken.

Washed over time, only maternal love remains.

Josiah Y.
Dulwich International High School Programme Hengqin

Morning Hero

Broom dances,
dust flies away.
Before sun wakes,
you start the day.

Trash bin smiles,
paper finds home.
Your shadow cleans
where kids will roam.

No cape, no mask -
just magic broom.
Our superhero
in morning gloom.

Kiki J.
Dulwich International High School Programme Hengqin

Mortal Wish

Mocking laughter falls into the pupils

Malicious stabbing of the heart

I am skilled at the ridicule and mockery of others

I grew up in a lonely and noisy world

I don't want to sit on thorns

Please help me

I don't want to fall into the abyss

Please help me

I expect my silence to be deafening

Please help me

When I met my own savior

Cut off the thorns that bind me

She heard my silent shout

Hold onto me

And

I am flying

She, coming like an angel

Reshaping my flawed heart

Like a dark night finally welcoming dawn

Like a displaced person finding a safe haven

Like people who have suffered from war finding utopia

I never prayed for her arrival

But she said,

I came for you

The gentle breeze swept over the hills

Ashes scattered chimes

I heard her say,

I live for you

Pyrotechnic world leisurely and lengthy

Love runs through the heart.

Rose Z.
Dulwich International High School Programme Suzhou

Mum

To me,

you are a delicious joyful donut

that I enjoy eating.

You are a sweet cute, glorious cat

that is so beautiful.

You are the smell of tasty sugarcane,

and the sound of wind blowing through the trees.

You are a light in the hollow forest

and my own sunrise of hope.

But best of all,

you are my mum.

Felix
Dehong Shanghai International Chinese School

My Everyday Superhero

My everyday superhero is tiny, but has a great power
Whenever I feel gloomy or joyful, my superhero stays by my side

Before I go to school,
My dog always sees me off in front of the house door
After I go back to my home,
My dog always welcomes me by wagging her tail

My everyday superhero is tiny, but has a great power
Whenever I feel depressed or delighted, my superhero stays by my side.

Ahin C.
Dulwich College Suzhou

My Friend

To me, you are tasty vanilla ice cream

That will never melt.

I enjoy the hours we spend together.

You are an elegant fox bringing plenty of feelings

And the wonderful smell of watery perfume.

You are the sound of scary loading music and a glass window shattering

Because we enjoy being scared together sometimes

You are a shining certificate in my hand and the feeling of being the champion of my music concert.

You are bright golden light that

Can wake me from any nightmare.

You are thoughts of forever

And my favourite music.

You are life itself.

Best of all, you are my friend.

Martina
Dehong Shanghai International Chinese School

My Hero Jane Goodall

Her hair was silver, her smile was warm.
At 90 years old, she stood on a chair so we all could see,
Though she was small, her words felt big to me.

She told us stories of forests and trees,
Of chimps she knew and the air they breathe.
Her hands moved gently as she spoke,
Like wind touching leaves, soft and slow.

This is not what a typical superhero looks like,
But her gentle and strong heart touched me deeply,
To let me realize a woman even so old can be a superhero,
As long as she cares so much and does her best.

I sang her song with my shy voice,
She nodded at me - that was enough.
No flashing lights or fancy tricks,
Just one kind lady who cares so much.

Now when I see a bird or a tree,
I stop and look... just like she taught me.

William W.
Dulwich College Beijing

My Little Brother

To me, you are a juicy mango, because you spill your sweetness into my heart.

You are a fearless dragon, because you step on a cloud and soar.

You are the scent of a rose among thorn bushes, because your family will always protect you.

And the sound of bells jingling against my bedroom door, taking me into my dreams.

You are the crystal trophy that is placed into my hand, because I will not forget how proud i am to have you.

You are the jade bracelet against my wrist, helping me remember the warmth of home through your coldness.

You are the galaxy that keeps me safe, always guiding me in the path of the Milky Way.

But best of all, you are my little brother.

Christine T.
Dehong Xi'an School

My Mum, The Town's Hero

I love my mom

My mom loves me back

She is always there for me

She protects me from bad guys

When bad guys appear

She karate-chops them

Punches them in the face

And kicks their legs

The bad guys fall

The bad guys beg for mercy

My mom is called the town's hero

Everyone claps

Everyone applauds

And everyone shouts, "Hip, hip, Hooray!"

After all her hard work is done

We go home

We talk about her accomplishments

And then go to bed

I love my mom

She loves me too

She is the town's hero

I hope she always will be.

Emily K.
Dulwich College Seoul

My Mother

To me, you are juicy strawberry ice cream
on a hot summer day
because you make me happy and joyful.
You are a powerful dragon
with enormous claws,
helping me when I am in trouble,
and a fluffy little sheep
calming me down
until the trouble has passed.
You are a beautiful, kind butterfly sat upon a rose bush,
the best butterfly in the world.
Your gentle voice
sounds like
my favorite song, sometimes
(when you are not angry).
You make me proud,
you are a trophy, a world cup.
You are a warm jacket,
making me feel safe.

You protect me from the dangers of this world, and who are you?

My mother,

and you deserve my thanks.

Amber
Dehong Shanghai International Chinese School

My Superhero

My superhero cannot fly

But he never leaves my hand when I cry

My superhero does not have a special power,

Neither can he jump from tower to tower,

My superhero is not so tall,

But he always catches me before I fall

My superhero does not keep a sword or shield

But he shines with pride in my small success in any field

He has turned into a hero by showing love and care,

A person who listens when I have problems

And I can always share it with,

Who does not allow me to be sad,

He will always be my superhero and I call him DAD.

Paula M.
Dulwich College Seoul

My Wonderful Brain

I am an intelligent brain.
Every day I help you think, see, balance and move.
I need to stand in your head every day.
I am so tired, I don't sleep or rest.
It's a very hard job to be a brain, don't you think?
I can't hear anything at all.
I can only taste blood because I am surrounded by your blood.

I am a secret superhero.
And I'm here to help you live your life.
If you trip, I will move your hands in front of you
And you won't get hurt.
I am here to save humanity!

Ruben M.L.
Dulwich College Seoul

Nurse Suzie & Doctor Brown

As a teen, I've been very sick,

Frequent visits to the clinic,

"You have that, it's a fact."

One shot here, one shot there,

"But tell me, Doctor Brown, is it fair?

Yes, I'm ill, yes, I'm cold,

But it feels as if you're leaching from my soul.

Is all of this really necessary?"

"Yes, of course," he said, "let me check your eyes,

Oh, and that will be 100 dollars, if you don't mind."

And so I reply,

"What about Nurse Suzie?

What does she think of all your tricks?

All you do is say and say but never give.

What about Nurse Suzie?

She's been so kind,

Instead of just you're fine!"

"When diagnosed with my issues,

She helped me through,

Not just because she's family,

Or for flattery.

She doesn't do anything dramatically,

Or for money,

Because Doctor Brown, last time I checked,

You aren't the one who finds people dead.

You never say the news, or try,

Just choose, just whine,

Slipping more in your pocket,

Gold dripping from your sockets.

So tell me, Doctor Brown, what about Nurse Suzie?"

Kira K.
Dulwich College Suzhou

Ordinary Superhero — Chocolate

Everyday superhero? Your wonders may cease.
But, a hero rises, wrapped in foil and grace.
It wields no blade, nor brings us peace,
Instead, it rescues our soul with a velvety hand.

From dark chocolate, rich and bold with its high cocoa might,
To milk chocolate, creamy and sweet, a tender sugary charm.
White chocolate glows, it's vanilla pure and bright in sight,
And ruby chocolate dances with berries, dazzling with its fruity alarm.
Together, they weave a sanctuary, a fanciful world,
Where every bite feels like an alchemy taking flight.

Yet, wait, and see its hidden plight -
"Is chocolate a villain, causing harm within?"
It's said to be a culprit, of weight and woe.
A sweet temptation, that we just can't let go.

But wait - there's more beneath the flavor of the alchemist,
In measured doses, it can heal, inspire, and motivate.

It melts away our worries, and wipes our weary minds.

It sparks moments of joy when our heart feels confined.

A gift to brighten each other's faces,

Where our love and energy leave traces.

Chocolate, a sanctuary, an alchemist,

Something that superheroes even seldom miss.

Joanna Q.
Dulwich College Shanghai Pudong

Paper Villain

I am the pain of your day,
A villain who can make your week gray,
I hide on your finger,
Waiting to strike.

People call me minor,
But little do they know,
I will burn you more than a lighter,
Can make the pain overflow.

I hid on your finger,
Waiting to strike,
Already waited on some paper,
Then I hitchhiked.

One droplet of water,
And pain strikes high,
You cry and cry,
But the pain still will not die.

Lumi L.
Dulwich College Seoul

Pencil Sharpener

I am a sneaky sharpener. HA HA HA!
I wait for where I can blend,
Touching and sharpening people's skin.
Each day, I see wooden pieces sharpened by me.
As sharp as a knife.
I feel the sharpened pencil and taste the pieces.
But there's more to me than that…

Evil comes in many secret ways.
Mine is hidden inside an object.
Mine is small and sharp.
I smell lots of hands, wrapped around my body.
I hear lots of sharpener friends… sharpening pencils.
Wait a second, It's your bare feet!
EEEEEEEOOOOOOWWWWW!!!
Perfect!

Jonathan S.
Dulwich College Suzhou

Police Officers

It's lucky that we have police officers

They keep out rioting "grrrrs"

If we didn't have them, who knows

Who would be there to stop murderers slicing off toes

There are police officers everywhere maintaining peace

In Ukraine, in Australia, you name it, in Greece

Criminals and killers and robbers alike

Police officers are what they dislike

"There's a bank robbery! Please help us!!!"

"The police are coming, no need to fuss!"

With a simple dial of 9-1-1

It will send baddies on the run.

Hanwen L.
Dulwich College Shanghai Pudong

Rude Sneaky Shower

I stand on the grabber.

I live in the bathroom.

Touching the wall.

I always hear people screaming loud,

Because of my cold breath and spit.

Each day I see people coming with their clothes off.

I sneak up and make my spit hot and cold!

I am a shower who is a secret villain!

I am here to make people scream.

"O………W! That stubborn shower!"

Because I am a top supervillain!

MUAHAHA!

I am going to make people scream out that my evil job!

And now I spit in the person's face!

HA HA HA!

Fantastic job to me!

Annie K.
Dulwich College Suzhou

Smile

A warm smile is a fay
That saves the day

It's just that warm smile
That cures your people

It lightens the dark
Knocks on their heart

In the bitter reality like coffee
Full of vileness

Drop some cubes of sugar
With those smiles

Open up the smooth, curved gate
It will change the people's fate.

Julie J.
Dulwich College Suzhou

Superhero

Sharing knowledge day by day

Using unique teaching methods

Patiently guiding your children every day

Encouraging us to find our way

Reminding us to try our best

Heart full of zeal, making dreams excel

Earnest showing, you never stop

Radiant beam in the life

Our teacher, you light up the night.

Aurora H.
Dulwich International High School Programme Hengqin

Superhero Next To Me

Soft eyes that hold a world of love,

Unwearyingly in her daily strive.

Patiently she mends each broken dream,

Endlessly giving, like a gentle stream.

Radiant with warmth through all our years,

Holding us close when doubt appears.

Ever-present in our every fear,

Rewarding us with love so dear.

Overflowing with grace, she lights our way.

Chanel C.
Dulwich International High School Programme Hengqin

Sweeper Of The Night

If you think about everyday heroes
One comes to mind
You may see them every day
Very easy to find
The wooden handled broom swings across the floor
This hard-working person, you might not think for
Humankind needs them like the Earth needs a core
They help all of the people, no matter rich or poor

As they work silently in the corner
They may not be born a tireless janitor
But without them, places wouldn't be liveable
And instead we sometimes make them invisible

In the day and the night, they keep daily life rolling
The dust is gone like pins in a game of bowling
They make the school halls and the malls shine with gleam
Every single job including cleaners has their theme.

Rowan T.
Dulwich College Suzhou

Teacher

Teachers are like the spring breeze
The knowledge I get is as deep as the sea.
We are like the nesting bird

Teachers hold you towards the sky
No matter how far you travel
No matter how long you haven't seen them
Their teaching still remains in my mind
I am glad to be a student
I am glad to be taught.

Sarah Z.
Dulwich College Suzhou

Terror

Neon lights, streets cold,
Footsteps loud, tales untold.
Midnight lingers, forever in time,
Shadows chase a story once mine.

City lights can't drown the ache,
Heartbeats slow, but won't quite break.
Memories whisper, pull me back,
Tracing steps along the map.

Fading echoes, empty space,
Longing for a lost embrace.
Dawn will rise, but still I roam,
Chasing it that won't come home.

Isaac H.
Dulwich College Shanghai Pudong

The Book

I am a very evil book.
I lie in wait for a person to pass by.
Touching a wall, a wooden bookshelf.
Each day I see people coming towards the bookshelf,
But then they just walk away.
I smell the dampness of the bookshelf, the dust on the bookshelf
And taste the musty air of this old rotten bookshelf.
I hear some people talking, I hear other books.
I taste the sour wood... dust and air.

But there is more to me than that.
I am a harmful, hurtful book, hard and fast.
And I am here to fall on you!
I will fall and break the people,
and hurt them with my sharp sides.
The humans will cry and shout – all for me to stop.
They will run away from me – RRUUNNNNNNN!
Excellent!

Julia S.
Dulwich College Suzhou

The Day Kindness Came To Visit

Kindness is something we usually can not see

But she is my friend,

She is gentle and she never gives up.

I had wanted to spend the day without her

I was playing computer games

And making a mess

With my headphones on

When

KNOCK. KNOCK. KNOCK.

She appeared at my door.

Kindness spoke softly and asked to come inside.

I wasn't sure, but then, Wow!

She had brought me a gift!

In a huge colorful box

My favorite robot,

How did she know I wanted this?

Together, we turned off my computer game

And tidied the sitting room.
She helped me - like a mother protecting her child.
We'd nearly finished when I found her feeding a street cat
With a sweet smile on her face.

I wished that she was free to feed all animals
And not just here with me.

After helping the cat we were hungry,
So we ate cheese sandwiches
And drank delicious juice.
We shared and laughed
And chatted
And made plans to help other people.
When it was time to say goodbye
I didn't go back to my computer game.

I went to collect donations
For other animals on the street.

Lucas
Dehong Shanghai International Chinese School

The Day That Bravery Came To Visit

Bravery, he is a man in silver armor. a hero riding a giant dragon.
One day he zoomed to my house.
His face battered
and bruised
from all his adventures.

I heard a strange sound
coming from the roof.
Then bursting through
the chimney
like a much less cheerful Santa Claus.
Was Bravery.
I felt surprised and scared
I am not used to being brave.
But he took me to the roof,
where his dragon snorted
full of energy.

"Come with us," Bravery said.
He pulled me onto the dragon.

Together we flew
over dangerous volcanoes
and mysterious rainforests.
Our fingertips skidded across the lake.
I saw fish jump into the shining sun.
Bravery caught one in his hand
and ate it raw.
I laughed
but did not try it.
I was scared of food poisoning, after all.

When we returned to the city
we saw adults having picnics
They panicked and ran to hide.
Perhaps they needed bravery of their own?

To remember our time together,
Bravery gave me a colourful scale,
the color of the rainbow
because Bravery is in everything
and everyone
if you look hard enough.

The next time Bravery comes to visit

Perhaps I will eat that fish.

Or perhaps we will adventure

in the rainforest.

Elsa
Dehong Shanghai International Chinese School

The Door Holder

She is known as the woman in crimson.
The bellhop in black.
And most notably the door holder.
It is a harder job than rolling Sisyphus's boulder.
She is consistent, reliable and the unsung hero who keeps the world spinning.
Never failing.
Unfortunately, someone as important as her is also the victim of abuse, verbal, physical and emotional.
But her unwavering determination to please the unappreciative public is what is truly impressive.
So, we should be appreciative.
Say our thanks and greetings.
It will make her so happy she will practically be beaming with joy.
Our slight gratitude will make all her troubles worth all her time.
Even if you are a young boy.
Or an old mime.
Just give her some recognition.
Give them all some recognition.

Neil A.
Dulwich College Seoul

The Evil Rubber

I am an evil rubber

I want to be evil because kids are always throwing and catching me!

I hate it!

So I am going to destroy the world!

I mean one kid

Oh look! Someone is drawing!

Rub, rub, rub.

"Nooooo!"

Perfect!

Now let's get some more people to be sad. Ha ha ha!

Lyra J.
Dulwich College Seoul

The Family's Embrace

In moments of struggle, when spirits wane,
They stand beside us through thick and thin.
With love as armor against all pain,
Their quiet strength helps us begin again.

Everyday heroes walk among us still,
In simple acts that often go unseen.
Their quiet courage bends to our will,
Making life brighter with each routine.

So let us honor those who serve and care,
With gratitude for their selfless ways.
For in each heart beats a hero rare,
Transforming our lives in countless ways.

Andrea R.
Dulwich College Shanghai Puxi

The Heroes That Walk With Us

Heroes walk with us

Each going about their day

Until we need help

The changes that they help make

Things they do for us

The stories that go untold

So, I give them thanks

To heroes that walk with us.

Michelle B.
Dulwich College Shanghai Puxi

The Ring

I'm a beautiful ring.

I wait on the desk touching a pencil.

Each day, I see children wearing me.

I hear children say, "Wow!"

I feel the children's fingers and taste old rings and new rings.

But there's more to me than that.

I am good and evil.

And I'm here to make you shiny.

I will make you beautiful and make your finger hurt.

The humans will throw me into a river and go away.

The whole house will run from my shining.

And I will feel...

Perfect!

Cheawon L., Joy B. and Seoyun J.
Dulwich College Suzhou

The Saviour Of The Stomach

Every day he drives his motor, people demand him to be faster.

His job is to be a lifesaver, to save people from the jaws of hunger.

He travels at the speed of thunder, to make their bellies feel much better.

In the eyes of poor and hungry youngsters, he's like an angel from the heavenly layer.

The things he carries are precious treasures, each has the price of silver.

It's him, it's him, it's definitely him!

The great and legendary food deliverer.

Cindy Z., Sally L. and Zoe H.
Dehong Xi'an School

The Window

I am a big window, I live on the window frame.

Touching the frame, waiting to magnify the light.

Every day I see the sun and people and tape,

Nothing I see is important except the sun, and my job's done.

I hear birds, I taste tape and paper

And I smell the air with smoke,

But, there's more to me than that…

I'm a villain and the evil sort,

I shine the magnified light in your eyes.

"Too bright!"

That's what you'll say,

The same happened to other people.

"Ah!" screamed some.

Some eye me, but that doesn't stop me and it is…

FANTASTIC.

Andrew L.
Dulwich College Seoul

They Were Everything To You

It started off so fun
As they welcomed you under the sun
And you knew through and through
That they were everything to you

Now you feel like you're going to crack
Now you think they don't care one bit
Now you spend your nights turning your back
But you don't realise they're the only ones who truly have it

They give so much
Yet all they want is for you to try
But even as such
You shout, you scream, you cry
And you forget one day you'll have to say goodbye

And as you leave and grow
You forget they could possibly ever go
But then there's a message on your phone
Saying "Darling, please come home."

So take back the tears
And instead spend your years
Smiling and playing and laughing
Or doing something as simple as saying
"I love you"
And this time remember why
They were everything to you

Theo G.
Dulwich College Shanghai Pudong

To Be Kind

Kind people live in kindness world.

Ignoble people will be arrested.

No act of kindness is ever wasted.

Daring to show kindness is always rewarded.

Noxious and dreaded, the problem loomed.

Everyone can be a superhero.

Sent people help because they need it.

Superhero might be every single person in this kindness world.

Amy Y.
Dulwich International High School Programme Hengqin

Upstanders

When you've lost your way
You shouldn't have to pay
Just take a breath and say
"I will not just think okay!"

You have to fight back
Say, "NO!"
"I don't believe that!"

"I don't believe in bullying,
I don't believe in being mean.
I don't believe in using someone
Then ditching them as queen."

You know that it's not right
And that's just the honest truth
You've got to turn away
You shouldn't do this another day

Don't hide in shame
Or cower and blame
You have to at least

be strong, for today

So when you see a person alone
Don't ever have a heart of stone
Ask, "Hey, are you lonely?
Do you want my company?"

That night, when you get home
You will spend some time alone
And realize a warm feeling
Spreading, and tingling

That's the feeling you'll get
When you do something you won't regret

Imagine a chestnut
Or a walnut or a coconut
As every person in the world

Coconuts, the hardest to crack - befriend
And walnuts the softest - hard to offend.
When you spend time a little with them
You will most definitely become sort of friends

Their shells may shudder
Become a little softer
And you might peek inside
For some short periods of time

The shell is an outside coating
A mask of their inner coding
Once, if you break through
The amazing shall be revealed

For the chestnut it's the nut
For the coconut it's the water
And the walnut the crunchy in-between

'Cause you see
Everyone is special
Everyone has potential
So listen, don't judge
Be as friendly as fudge
And they won't refuse or budge.

Isabel L.
Dulwich College Shanghai Pudong

War

If I know how to cook,

I will give homeless people a taste of home.

I will change the smoke of war to the smoke that led to home.

If I know how to cook,

I will make the world into a huge restaurant.

People forget their worries and enjoy the moment,

Turn the restaurant into a Michelin.

Therefore, I could hear the laughter of children again.

If I know how to cook,

I will smash the potato into one piece.

Elizabeth S.
Dulwich College Suzhou

Way

When we are walking in our life way

We feel drowned under the sea

We are wrong

Try to lift your head

There are many saviours around you

They will always try to save you

They will always stay in front of you

When we are walking in our life way

We are not alone

While we dropped our head

Waves come to our life

Until we reach the end.

Felix K.
Dulwich College Suzhou

Xi'an

I'm from a place where I go to the park,
In the park I can see some butterflies,
I can hear birds singing,
I can smell new flowers.

I'm from a place where I can eat local food,
I can see lots of Xi'an's traditional food,
I can hear cooks talking,
I can smell the food sizzling.

I'm from a place that has so much history,
I can see many cultural buildings,
I can hear guides introduce local historical relics,
I can smell the taste of the changing times.

Hannah S.
Dehong Xi'an School

Yes Indeed, Things We Need

Plants are necessary, yes indeed,

They make the sorrowful feel glee.

Animals are so cute, yes indeed,

They make people feel happy.

The weather is helpful, yes indeed,

They help the farmers harvest feed.

Parents are so great, yes indeed,

They help their children with their needs.

Every person's important, yes indeed,

They help others with their deeds.

Every tiny little thing

Is so important - yes, indeed!

Horace G. and Martin Z.
Dehong Xi'an School

Your Own Hero

When you hear "superhero",
who do you see?
A parent, a friend, or someone from the movies,
or someone full of empathy?
But there's a hero,
where everyone knows,
someone within you,
a force all your own.

When darkness falls,
and hope seems thin and distant,
you've been your own light
persisting, intense, resistant.
Through every stumble,
through every heavy climb,
you've cherished your dreams
with love over time.
You've always been your own hero.

Liya D.
Dulwich International High School Programme Hengqin

www.ingramcontent.com/pod-product-compliance
Lightning Source LLC
Chambersburg PA
CBHW042044280426
43661CB00094B/1003